Edinburgh Castle

by Grace Hansen

abdobooks.com

Published by Abdo Kids, a division of ABDO, P.O. Box 398166, Minneapolis, Minnesota 55439.
Copyright © 2022 by Abdo Consulting Group, Inc. International copyrights reserved in all countries.
No part of this book may be reproduced in any form without written permission from the publisher.
Abdo Kids Jumbo™ is a trademark and logo of Abdo Kids.

Printed in the United States of America, North Mankato, Minnesota.

052021

092021

Photo Credits: Alamy, Getty Images, Granger Collection, iStock, Shutterstock

Production Contributors: Teddy Borth, Jennie Forsberg, Grace Hansen
Design Contributors: Candice Keimig, Pakou Moua

Library of Congress Control Number: 2020947581
Publisher's Cataloging-in-Publication Data

Names: Hansen, Grace, author.

Title: Edinburgh castle / by Grace Hansen

Description: Minneapolis, Minnesota : Abdo Kids, 2022 | Series: Famous castles | Includes online resources
and index.

Identifiers: ISBN 9781098207298 (lib. bdg.) | ISBN 9781098208134 (ebook) | ISBN 9781098208554
(Read-to-Me ebook)

Subjects: LCSH: Edinburgh Castle (Edinburgh, Scotland)--Juvenile literature. | Castles--Juvenile literature. |
Architecture--Juvenile literature.

Classification: DDC 728.81--dc23

Table of Contents

Fortress on Castle Rock

Edinburgh Castle soars over the capital city of Scotland. The fortress was built on Castle Rock, a 460-foot-high (140 m) hill.

Scotland
Edinburgh
Europe
N
W
E
S

Humans have occupied Castle Rock for more than 3,000 years. Kings and queens have lived there since Malcolm III in the 1000s CE.

Malcolm III

Edinburgh Castle's location is one of power. It is one of the most important fortresses in Scotland. Because of this, the castle has been a part of many battles. It is one of the most attacked places in the world.

One such fight took place during the **War of Independence**. In 1314, Sir Thomas Randolph led the Scots through the castle in a nighttime raid. They retook the castle from the English who had held it for 20 years.

11

Changes Over the Years

Many kings and queens left their mark at Edinburgh Castle. Queen Margaret died there in 1093. Her son, David I, built a chapel in her honor. Today it is one of the oldest buildings in all of Scotland.

Queen Margaret

In 1511, King James IV completed
the Great Hall. The grand space
held many **royal** events over
the years.

14

15

Above the door to the Royal Palace are the initials MAH. The initials are for Mary, Queen of Scots, and her husband Henry. James VI, Mary's son, was born in the castle in 1566. His **reign** would unite Scotland and England.

Mary with James VI
15 66

Royals rarely came to the castle after the **Union of the Crowns** in 1603. Beginning in the 1650s, the castle went back to its roots. It became an important military base. It also served as a prison until 1814.

The Castle Today

The military still uses the castle today. It is also a popular place to visit. The Crown Room holds the castle's most valued treasures. There visitors can see the **Honours of Scotland** and the **Stone of Destiny**.

Queen Elizabeth II
Honours of Scotland

More Facts

- Castle Rock, which Edinburgh Castle sits atop, was formed by volcanic activity that took place 340 million years ago!

- King James IV did not get to enjoy The Great Hall for long. Two years after it was completed, he died at the Battle of Flodden in 1513.

- Edinburgh Castle hosts more than 1 million visitors each year.

Glossary

Honours of Scotland – also known as the Scottish Crown Jewels, the crown, scepter, and sword used in ceremonies to crown new kings and queens.

reign – rule by a king or queen.

royal – of or having to do with a king or queen, or any members of their family.

Stone of Destiny – a large piece of red sandstone used during crowning ceremonies and an ancient symbol of Scotland's monarchy.

Union of the Crowns – the moment James VI, King of Scotland (cousin and only heir of Elizabeth I of England) also became King James I of England.

War of Independence – in Scotland, a series of military campaigns fought between the Kingdom of Scotland and the Kingdom of England in the late 13th and early 14th centuries.

Index

Visit **abdokids.com** to access crafts, games, videos, and more!